KEEPING MUM

Books by Gwyneth Lewis

POETRY IN WELSH

Sonedau Redsa (Gwasg Gomer, 1990)
Cyfrif Un ac Un yn Dri (Cyhoeddiadau Barddas, 1996)
Y Llofrudd Iaith (Cyhoeddiadau Barddas, 1999)

POETRY IN ENGLISH

Parables & Faxes (Bloodaxe Books, 1995)
Zero Gravity (Bloodaxe Books, 1998)
Keeping Mum (Bloodaxe Books, 2003)

PROSE

Sunbathing in the Rain: A Cheerful Book about Depression
(Flamingo, 2002)

GWYNETH LEWIS

KEEPING MUM

BLOODAXE BOOKS

ISBN: 1 85224 583 2

First published 2003 by
Bloodaxe Books Ltd,
Highgreen,
Tarset,
Northumberland NE48 1RP.

www.bloodaxebooks.com
For further information about Bloodaxe titles
please visit our website or write to
the above address for a catalogue.

Bloodaxe Books Ltd acknowledges
the financial assistance of
Arts Council England, North East.

Cover printing by J. Thomson Colour Printers Ltd, Glasgow.

Printed in Great Britain by
Cromwell Press Ltd, Trowbridge, Wiltshire.

To Leighton
of course

ACKNOWLEDGEMENTS

Poems in this collection have previously appeared in *Metre*, *Poetry London*, *Poetry Wales* and *Quadrant*.

I would like to acknowledge Barddas, publisher of *Y Llofrudd Iaith* in 1999 and Richard Poole for his translation of 'Her End'.

I'm grateful to the City of London Festival for permission to publish *Chaotic Angels*, poems commissioned for the Angel Series of concerts in 2002.

I am extremely grateful to NESTA for its support. The National Endowment for Science, Technology and the Arts awarded me a five-year fellowship in 2001.

CONTENTS

PREFACE

I live a double life. I was brought up speaking a language which predates the Roman invasion of Britain. When I'm frightened I swear in ancient Brythonic idioms. Yet I'm a city dweller, and surf the net using the language of the Saxons who pushed the Welsh into the hills of western Britain in the sixth century. I write in both languages. It's a difficult domestic arrangement, but it holds.

One of my survival tactics until now has been to keep both sides of my linguistic family apart for as long as possible. I publish one book in Welsh, the next in English. Translating my own work from Welsh into English has held little appeal, simply because the audience and concerns addressed are distinct and, often, mutually antagonistic. Also, I dislike repeating myself.

The death of the Welsh language has been predicted for many centuries. With devolution some political optimists declared that the battle for the language had been won. I disagree, having seen my grandparents' village changing from being virtually monoglot Welsh to being a rural community which will have more in common with the Lake District or the Yorkshire Dales than with its own past in the Cambrian mountains. If the language is dying it seems important to know who or what killed it.

In 1999 I wrote a book-length detective story investigating the murder of my mother tongue, calling it *Y Llofrudd Iaith*, 'The Language Murderer'. The plot of the original book was set in a West Wales village, where an old lady, my embodiment of the Welsh language, had been found dead. In the book as a whole I wanted to explore how we could free ourselves of the idea of a "mother tongue" with all its accompanying psychological baggage and its infantilising of native speakers. Detective Carma, half-Welsh, half-Japanese, was the investigating officer and I'm not going to tell you the outcome.

Can you imagine having to speak Spanish for the rest of your life because everybody else around you has stopped speaking English at home? The prospect of losing a whole culture is an existential nightmare for a Welsh-speaker, fraught with questions of one's own responsibility in preserving collective values without becoming a parrot for the past. To most English speakers, it can't seem any more important than the loss of Morris dancing. I was persuaded, however, that the fate of a language might be of interest to those

9

concerned with the wider linguistic ecology – after all, if endangered plants offer cures for cancer, what essential directions might be hidden in obscure Welsh proverbs about never ploughing at a run?

The first section of *Keeping Mum* represents as much of *The Language Murderer* as I was able to translate in a fairly direct fashion. Only a handful of the poems are literal versions. Richard Poole translated 'Her End' in consultation with me. Revisiting the subject stimulated entirely new poems in English, and I allowed those to take shape. These are translations without an original text – perhaps a useful definition of poetry.

Section two of this book is a more radical recasting of my original detective story and a meditation on mental illness and language. In his essay on poetry and psychoanalysis in *Promises, Promises*, Adam Phillips quotes Lacan echoing Freud: 'Psychoanalysis should be the science of language inhabited by the subject. From the Freudian point of view man is the subject captured and tortured by language.' My translated detective was to be a psychiatrist in a mental hospital, investigating how abuses of language had led to his patients' illnesses.

Therapy's based on the premise that an accurate description of a situation releases the patient from being neurotically bound to it. Psychoanalysts have even more faith in language than do poets. In the face of experience our explanations always break down. Far from being a failure, however, this wordlessness is usually a clue that something more truthful than our own account of the world is being approached: the 'keeping mum' of this book's title.

The third section of the book, *Chaotic Angels*, looks at communications between different realms of awareness. Commissioned by Kathryn McDowell, Director of the City of London Festival for the Angel Series of concerts in 2002, the sonnets were written to match Dragan Andjelic's canvases exhibited in the Wren churches of the City. They focus on angels as messengers from another realm. I use the language of modern Chaos Theory to re-imagine angels as part of our everyday lives – at the centre of experiences like depression and bereavement.

Detective, psychiatrist, angel – the sequence of communicators leads out ever further, in the service of a clarity which is not my own.

I

The Language Murderer

POLICE FILE

A Poet's Confession

'I did it. I killed my mother tongue.
I shouldn't have left her
there on her own.
All I wanted was a bit of fun
with another body
but now that she's gone –
it's a terrible silence.

She was highly strung,
quite possibly jealous.
After all, I'm young
and she, the beauty,
had become a crone
despite all the surgery.

Could I have saved her?
made her feel at home?

Without her reproaches.
I feel so numb,
not free, as I'd thought…

Tell my lawyer to come.
Until he's with me,
I'm keeping mum.'

What's in a Name?

Today the wagtail finally forgot
that I once called it *sigl-di-gwt*.

It didn't give a tinker's toss,
kept right on rooting in river moss,

(no longer *mwswgl*) relieved, perhaps,
that someone would be noticing less

about its habits. Magpies' fear of men
lessened, as we'd lost one means

(the word *pioden*) of keeping track
of terrorist birds out in the back.

Lleian wen is not the same as 'smew'
because it's another point of view,

another bird. There's been a cull:
gwylan's gone and we're left with 'gull'

and blunter senses till that day
when 'swallows', like *gwennol*, might stay away.

Mother Tongue

'I started to translate in seventy-three
in the schoolyard. For a bit of fun
to begin with – the occasional "fuck"
for the bite of another language's smoke
at the back of my throat, its bitter chemicals.
Soon I was hooked on whole sentences
behind the shed, and lessons in Welsh
seemed very boring. I started on print,
Jeeves & Wooster, Dick Francis, James Bond,
in Welsh covers. That worked for a while
until Mam discovered Jean Plaidy inside
a Welsh concordance one Sunday night.
There were ructions: a language, she screamed,
should be for a lifetime. Too late for me.
Soon I was snorting Simenon
and Flaubert. Had to read much more
for any effect. One night I OD'd
after reading far too much Proust.
I came to, but it scared me. For a while
I went Welsh-only but it was bland
and my taste was changing. Before too long
I was back on translating, found that three
languages weren't enough. The "ch"
in German was easy, Rilke a buzz...
For a language fetishist like me
sex is part of the problem. Umlauts make me sweat,
so I need a multilingual man
but they're rare in West Wales and tend to be
married already. If only I'd kept
myself much purer, with simpler tastes,
the Welsh might be living...
                              Detective, you speak
Russian, I hear, and Japanese.
Could you whisper some softly?
I'm begging you. Please...'

Farm Visit

Each cow has a hairstyle
and walks in high heels,
bearing a handbag – the reticulum,
in which she transports her chewing gum.

They lick their nostrils
with liquorish tongues.
'You like that, detective? Never turn
your back on a cow or assume she's tame.

My mother was trampled,
had to be pulled
free from the herd.' The kodak field
was suddenly filled

with black and white Holsteins
like standing stones
around us, their sileage breath
sweet, oppressive. 'Your sister confessed...'

'This village had already died.
One prion, detective, has killed a trade:
the butcher wielding his favourite knife,
a food chain. A language. A way of life.'

Suddenly a restless cow reared,
starting a huffing stampede
towards us. Shouting, the farmer tore
a heifer aside by her jigsaw ear,

and, holding me roughly by the hand,
showed me how to stand my ground.
We played musical statues with the herd,
which froze every time he uttered a word.

Home Cooking

'I thought she was magic. Like the time
we went to pick *llysiau duon bach*
up on the mountain. I rolled the fruit
carefully between finger and thumb,
pleased with the patina that made them look
like mineral berries sweated out
of bitter bedrock. I heard a shout

and my mother said she'd see us back
at the house. We were ling-di-long,
stopped at the quarry to throw stones...
When we got in, a cooling rack
held two steaming pies, the washing-up done.
I was stunned and couldn't work out
how her time had gone slower. 'Short cut,'

they told me. But a lift
was the real answer. Then I knew
that mothers didn't live in straight lines.
Her world was folded, she had a gift
for swiftness, sweetness and for telling lies.
My faith in directness was undermined.
I was always the plodder, a long way behind.'

llysiau duon bach: bilberries

Small Holding

Last light on the hilltops and his crop of stones
is ripening nicely. It's time he trashed
my grandfather's hedgerows of beech,
pleached them against the rustling rain.
'I haven't been down to the village again

since the night of the concert. I keep
myself to myself. I take it you've heard
the rumours of big cats hunting sheep.
Ask about killing the already dead
and the beast of prey inside the head.'

'My father was distant...'

'Faced with perpetual winter in the house
he turned his attention, the greater part of love,
outside and kept a daily Weather Book,
an act of faith that things were on the move,
despair can change. His neat Remarks

show him a connoisseur of Wet
in months so boring I suspect a code
in "Fair but rather sultry in the E",
and "Wintry showers", outlined in red.
The highlight is: "A cloudburst in Cwmdu,

extensive damage caused." It's plain –
a light, then gentler, later stiffening breeze,
a week in July of "very BRIGHT".
No comments then for several days.
He was an adulterer with light.'

A Past

Don't look. But see that mountain there?
I've had sex with her often.
Now we're only friends
but, God, I was very fond of her,

spent many an active afternoon
in her secret crannies,
hiking, sweating.
She liked me alone,

wouldn't tolerate company
(a jealous mountain).
I once took a gang
to see her, but she'd have none of me

pulled up her B roads, made a mist
to hide herself from us.
We ended up
stuck in a farmer's ditch. What a bitch!

Her End

'The end was dreadful. Inside a dam burst
and blood was everywhere. Out of her mouth
came torrents of words, *da yw dant*
i atal tafod, gogoniannau'r Tad
in scarlet flowers – *yn Abercuawg*
yd ganant gogau – the blood was black,
full of filth, a well that amazed
with its vivid idioms – *bola'n holi ble mae 'ngheg?* –
and always fertile, *yes no pwdin llo*,
and psalms were gathering in her viscera
and gushing out of her, proverbs, coined words,
the names of plants, seven types of gnat,
dragonfly, rosemary, mountain ash,
then disgusting pus, and long-lost terms
like *gwelltor* and *rhychor*, her vomit a road
leading away from her, a force
leaving the fortress of her breath,
gwyr a aeth Gatráeth.
And after the crisis, nothing to be done
but watch her die, as saliva and sweat
of words poured out like ants   *padell pen-glin,*
Anghydffurfiaeth, clefyd y paill,
and, in spite of our efforts, in the grey of dawn
the haemorrhage ended, her lips were white,
the odd drop splashing. Then she was gone.'

Da yw dant i atal tafod: A tooth is a good barrier for the tongue; *gogoniannau'r Tad:* the Father's glories; *yn abercuawg yd ganant gogau:* cuckoos sing in Abercuawg (from a 9th-century poem); *bola'n holi, ble mae 'ngheg:* my stomach asking where my mouth is; *yes no pwdin llo:* yes, no, calf's pudding (a nonsensical phrase); *gwelltor* and *rhychor:* the left- and right-hand oxen in a ploughing pair; *gwyr a aeth Gatráeth:* men went to Catraeth (from Aneirin's 6th-century poem, *Y Gododdin*); *padell pen-glin:* kneecap; *Anghydffurfiaeth:* Nonconformity; *clefyd y paill:* hay fever.

Aphasia

I ask for 'hammer' but am given 'spade',
feel like some 'tea' but order 'orangeade'

by mistake. I specify 'velvet' but am given 'silk'
in a colour I don't even like

but I take it, pretend. Someone's cut the string
between each word and its matching thing,

so my mind's a junk shop of where I've been.
I'll never know now what I really mean.

Brainstorming

What if I slept tonight beside Taliesin's stone
to solve the murder? Would it send me mad,
or make me a poet? It must be remade

daily, this moorland, as it is destroyed
each time we leave it. See it shake
with wind that knocks the noisy larks

off their high pillars. Even they fall
in silence. I need to know
what survives forgetting. The shadow

grown here but never harvested?
The hillside's humming? I could pray
to know this tumultuous energy

before it falls into pools, then streams
down to the valley into livestock, names,
marriages, murders and on into time.

Forget forgetting. Will I survive
the lichen hissing like flying spray,
the mountain wave under me giving way?

Taliesin: the 6th-century poet who later became a mythical figure and shape-shifter. His stone, in Cardiganshire, is reputed either to drive people who sleep there mad or turn them into poets.

II

Keeping Mum

MEMOIRS OF
A PSYCHIATRIST

Lifesaving for Psychiatrists

Of course, it's violent. The apparently drowned
have a grip that's deadly. To master a man,
practise the different breaks on dry land;

bring up your knee to his groin;
on his throat you can use your palms,
or press his eyeballs in with your thumbs

till you're the master. It looks like sex
or a tango. Gaining the upper hand
in water is beautiful and reminds

the cultured observer of Beatrice
and Dante floating in Paradise,
buoyant and easy. Face to face

with a drowned man, never promise
that you can save him.
That depends on the kiss.

Consultant

I am the one who makes the statues move,
who teaches the dead to rise and love

again, more wisely. I help the damned
explore what happened, who condemned

them each to their particular hell.
Yes, I'm in favour of using pills,

but my main job is to translate
pain into tales they can tolerate

in another language. We've pleasant grounds.
Care to come with me on my rounds?

Dissociation

CASE TAPES

Miss D

'On the pavilion
rain's small hands
tap braille on the windows.
I don't understand:

Someone was killed here,
but no one will tell.
I watch as patients
play games of bowls,

rolling wood planets
under sighing trees.
That corpse I mentioned?
I think it's me.'

Early Days in Psychiatry

Before the arrival of modern medicines
patients were frozen like statuary,
condemned to act the seven deadly sins
in tableaux of torment. We set some free

with lithium (remember Lot's wife?
her salt helps the heavy).
Even the barbarous ECT
seemed like a miracle. Rural life

was a nightmare. We'd find
children kept in chicken sheds
rocking like roosters, out of their minds
with neglect. A boy, half dead,

chained like a dog. Although we freed
his body, we never touched the fear
that held him – a stronger, invisible lead –
to that stinking farmyard. We'd hear

whispers of incest and often see
moon faces in windows, hurriedly withdrawn.
But I learned their code of secrecy,
listened at hedges and prescribed to thorns.

Finding the Bodies

DREAM WORK

Miss D

'Last night I dug up my father's vegetable patch
in Bridge Street, by the old swing.
"You always have to dig in the end,
I've put this off for far too long,"
I said to myself. The dead
– no, the murdered – are given a tent
where their body's located, an official camp
for the start of enquiries. I made a note
to tell the shrink that an underground stream
ran from left to right across the plot.
"We'll have asparagus from that," I thought.'

Tongue Fetishist

I've had two Christs already this year
one Hitler and a Mother of God
in my private clinic. I spend my time
listening to them, making things clear,
pointing to any suggestive rhymes

that might lead to reason.
Sense almost always follows sound,
so I've found. I speak
six languages, so keeping mum
isn't an option, but I'm a freak...

That book is my *Atlas of the Tongue*,
shows you diseases of the mouth,
fungus and tumours, how to take care
of the flesh for talking. Yours, my dear,
is remarkable. Come closer. Say Aah...

A Teenage Craze

'Curious, one day, about the other side,
I made friends with an "Englie" behind the shed.

Like "Welshies", they played by the railway track,
counted coal trucks as they passed

until we were giddy. Then we picked
sticky honeysuckle bracts

and she showed me how to pinch and pull
the flower's filament through its style

and place the nectar drop on my tongue,
a vaccine for sweetness. It all came undone

for no reason in the toilets one day
when the game turned into strangling me

for treason. I didn't think to resist
as the walls went screechy. I tasted rust

from the fire in my gullet, because I knew
it wasn't personal, but a clue

to the trap that was sprung inside my throat
just waiting to catch me. So I kept

my eyes wide open, though my vision bruised,
and I watched as I died, mildly amused

by the fear in my murderer's eyes. That grew
till the monoglot girl had to let me go

because her nerve failed her. I was nearly dead.
But I was the one with the rush to the head.'

Therapy

Did you hear the one about the shrink
who let obsessive-compulsives clean his house
as if their illnesses were his?
They made good caretakers, stayed up all night
rattling doorknobs, testing locks,
domesticated poltergeists.

He started an amateur dramatics group
with the psychotics, who had a ball
in togas, till they burnt down the hall.
Chronic depressives are always apart,
so he'd check them through his telescope,
placed them in poses from classical art

and, of course, they'd hardly ever move,
added a certain style to the grounds.
He recorded Tourette patients' sounds,
sold them to pop groups as backing tracks.
Whenever possible, he'd encourage love
between staff and patients. He had a knack

with manics, whom he sent out to shop
for all his parties, gave tarot cards
to schizoids so they could read their stars.
Perhaps he was flip with other people's pain
but his patients loved him and his hope
that two or three madnesses might make one sane.

A Promising Breakthrough

'You're right, I don't remember the egg
before it was broken. When it was whole,
as a word it filled my six-year-old palms,
oblong, complete and a little warm,
a gift for my mother. I recall the jolt –
a blue hydrangea as I bit my tongue –
pain in my marrow, not having hands
free to protect myself. The dog
came to lick up the horrible yolk
that oozed from my fingers, a shocking glue,
from the jagged jigsaw of shell.' Long pause. 'I felt
it was me who was broken because all my care
couldn't save my treasure'. Even longer spell.
'Egg doesn't always mean preciousness.
It was still an egg when it was a mess.'
'Oh God. Don't tell me. A lifetime's sense of loss
based on mistranslation?' 'That's entirely poss.'

Spread a Little Happiness

Now that millions are taking the pills
and pissing out Prozac, the salmon trout
are very much mellower and rivers run
with chemical happiness. My gift
to mosquitos is a blast of 'cool
head' that just takes the edge
off problems like dying. Mozzie, take a hit
of anti-depressant. I recommend it!

A Talent for Fainting

'First time I fainted I'd just told a lie
to the boy next door who'd come to play.
I'd said my name was Jenny.
It's not. I found a living bird
being eaten by ants. It sounds absurd,
but I quite like falling. They gave me pills
but that never stopped me, I could faint at will
fall gracefully, and always ended up draped
round someone compliant. There was a man
who said he was married to me and slept
in my bed. I don't recollect
a wedding but he was always kind
and good at catching. Where did I go
when my awareness left my mind?
Haven't the faintest. But I seem too old
for a woman who's barely lived a week
in twenty-six years. Doctor, how dare
you suggest it's a reaction to fear.
Whatever's wrong is much more rare
than common terror. Quickly, call
for someone stronger. I'm going to fall...'

Psychiatist, Twitcher

Words always return to the scene of the crime.
They have a legitimate point of view.
And I have mine.

You have to be patient, because speech is shy,
won't come if you're noisy,
or keep asking why.

I use my silence as a khaki hide
to flush out the wildlife.
I make tea inside,

have a textbook wish-list, hope for the rare
so I can tick it,
prove it was there.

Sometimes I catch the glint of an eye
in my binoculars –
in here, with me.

What is this presence that dares give chase
and me, a doctor?
My most dangerous case.

A Question

CASE NOTES
Miss D

'Doctor, do you think you can lose your soul?'
Miss D once asked me. I tried to stay cool
but the question shook me. 'I dreamt I was in hell,'
the patient continued, ignoring the dread
on my face. 'Although I was dead
my body continued, couldn't disappear
from the life of the living. Loved ones tore
my organs daily, unaware
that they broke my body by walking the streets.
At one point I became liquid dirt,
spattered and macerated into an ooze
a molecule thin but I couldn't lose
my consciousness. I felt everything:
the whole world tasted of nothing but shit,
I was shit incarnate because I felt it
in every particle of what had been me.
And I was a torturer too, for the guilty
had to hurt others – I was assigned
"soft duties" – hammering living bones
"till they stung but didn't ulcerate,"
said Quality Control. Rodin's Gates
of Hell were there, covered in gore,
and you had to look at them. There was more...
Doctor,' she asked again, 'can lose your soul?'

I'm not religious. Her despair
appalled me. Then I didn't dare
say 'Yes'. But knowing what I know now
I wish to God that I hadn't said 'No'.

Panic Attack

You've fallen through ice. Above you men
with ladders are sidling to where you fell in

to this cold cathedral with its shattered dome.
Ice has you in its picture frame

for a full-length portrait but minus breath.
Light doesn't help. Safety's underneath,

a little deeper, if only you dare
look up to the jagged dark. That's air,

shouts, dogs barking, warm hands and ropes.
Aim for the dark. It's your only hope.

Seaside Sanatorium

CASE TAPES
Miss D

'I live at a distance
from my own life,
a true provincial. That delay
has cost me everything.

Dogs search, frantic, for the thread
by which to unravel a slackening tide.
They never find it.

The ocean's a bore
with its circular breathing.
Light, also boring, moves up a gear
and a thrush cries "Cricket, wicket,"
everything twice.

"Start living," they say,
but I don't know how.
My life is a party
in another room
and I'm not invited.
I like my own gloom.

The nurses push you
to walk outside.
I prefer the skies
inside my head.

They'll all be sorry
when they find me dead.'

Night Passage to Nantucket

Those days night ferries travelled blind
and, once they were over Nantucket Bar,
used a single searchlight to pick out buoys
and find the channel. I sat outside,
watched the light swinging as if it could feel
the port side cans and starboard cones,
reading the fairway by floodlit braille.

My patients fumble for every word.
I refuse them the searchlight, sit on my hands
as they drift towards their most dangerous sands.
I must stay quiet. They have to learn
to distrust car headlights, that a landing star
is a plane. They need new marks
for self-navigation, to know where they are.

The Perfect Crime

CASE TAPES

Miss D

He killed her from fifteen years ago,
the perfect murder, with her own hands
and his suggestions about what she should be.
This poem doesn't rhyme but it's true.

It was a psychic slaying. His alibi
was watertight, he was already dead,
had left no fingerprints but lies –
all she wanted was to rhyme with him.

A delayed reaction meant that she took years
to see his meaning when he'd cut the ground
from under any of her future feet.
This poem isn't true but rhymes.

And then she got it: that she had no self
because she'd depended on his 'you',
and that was gone. She had to die.
This poem rhymes and is also true.

Retired Psychiatrist

Youngsters today don't speak semaphore
or even learn basic Morse Code any more.

The lightships are gone,
and their besweatered men

who watched seas for me. I used to know
where the occulting word-buoys were moored

but somebody's moved them – saboteurs
or my latest stroke. There is a tear

in the rip tide and I hear the roar
of the shoal that will wreck me, it's very near.

Across this estuary of lightest airs
others have hoisted spinnakers

of unearthly beauty and, silently,
glide out, like me, to the open sea.

Memorial Service
Miss D

Nothing anyone ever said helped.
She took up hobbies and even tried
to break with her mother, though she was dead.

For a while it seemed to be going so well.
She was optimistic, phoned me to tell
that she loved her courses. She was so frail

but no one can give their strength away
to carry another. Nothing I'd say
made any difference. At the end of the day

she just got tired. Hope takes work
and is exhausting. She drew a blank.
What chances have we if this girl sank?

What They Don't Teach You in Medical School

Guilt feels like love but never is.
Love feels like boredom because it's a home;
it offers excitement but mainly rest.
Ego's flamingo, but the common herd
is where your patients – even the best –
belong. Accusation's a front
for self-aggression. Help patients hunt
their monsters – make sure they're never your own –
to their shit-covered lairs. Beware
of omniscience, it makes a fool
of every psychiatrist. Play Virgil
to Dante as he walks through hell
then let him decide if he wants to be well.
You are the pagan who's outside the walls
of their paradise. You must bow your head
when you hear your Dante torn to shreds
by gods not your own. Many say no
to heaven. You must let them go.

III

Chaotic Angels

1 Pagan Angel

You ask me how it is we know
God's talking, not us. When even a stone
can photograph lilies and, as it falls,
prove that gravity's no more than speed?
When loquacious skies call
in gamma-rays, radio, infra-red,
and that's if we're not listening at all?

The heart's a chamber whose broody dead
stage pagan rituals. Wind blows
across stone lintels, making a tune
about absent bodies.
You ask me again:
'Where's the angel acoustic?'
My dear, the curlew. The quickening rain.

2 Tarot Angel

You can chase him through the Tarot de Marseilles.
Here is the Tower with its tumbling men
and crashing illusions. Take great care
as you decide what this all might mean:
that's His department. After all, we're scared
of the Death card and the Hanging Man
though what they signify is far from clear.

It has to be lived. Of course, we all die
but we live as though this weren't possible.
Who says this is folly? It might come true.
Step over the cliff with me, the Fool,
take a chance on changing. Die every day
as if you were living and that you knew
that broad roads score the blazing sky.

3 Fire Angel

For now it's music that holds up this church –
chromatic buttresses, a spandrel wall
of finest vibrato, while the spire
narrows to nothing on its rising scale,
leaving the weathercock to turn at will,
prompted by any weathery whim.
Melody, for once, has overcome fire.

But I've seen different. Led by a boy
who lit up plastic-bottle flares
and guided me, nervous, underground
in Acco, knowing that I should feel fear,
but I didn't and he led me far
into flickering vaults, a garrison
built by crusaders, remembered in flame.

4 Angels of Stage and Screen

Every actor in Hollywood knows
you have to keep still.
Don't wobble your head when talking to girls.
You let the action come to you.
Cultivate your charisma too,
mortify flesh in the latest gym.
These are the ways to become a star.

Angels are opposite. A modern kind
appears on radar, so sailors see
much deeper than distance. No 'Me, Me, Me',
these are messages without a source,
at least, to our knowledge. A crew stands awed,
surrounded by angel anomalies
dancing, invisible, on a flat-calm sea.

5 Minimal Angel

The smallest angel of which we're aware
is a 'spinning nothing'. Angel of dust,
angel of stem cells, of pollen grains,
angel of branches which divide to a blur
as they're ready to bud, becoming more
than their sum was even an hour before.
Angel of dog smells, angels of stairs,

of gardening, marriage. Cherubim
of rotting rubbish, of seeing far,
of rain's paste diamonds after a shower.
Radiation angels, angels of mud,
angels of slowing and of changing gear,
angels of roundabouts, and of being here
all say: 'You were made for this – prayer.'

6 Angel of Depression

Why would an angel choose to come here
if it weren't important? Into stuffy rooms
smelling of cabbage? Into the tedium of time,
which weighs like gravity on any messenger
used to more freedom and who has to wear
a dingy costume, so as not to scare
the humans. Wouldn't even an angel despair?

Don't say it's an honour to have fought
with depression's angel. It always wears
the face of my loved ones as it tears
the breath from my solar plexus, grinds
my face in the ever-resilient dirt.
Oh yes, I'm broken but my limp
is the best part of me. And the way I hurt.

7 How to Read Angels

Yes, information, but that's never all,
there's some service, a message. A lie dispelled,
something forgiven, an alternative world
glimpsed, for a moment, what you wanted to hear
but never thought possible. You feel a fool
but do something anyway and are filled
with delight as you unfold

like a wing in a thermal. If it's peace
you're left with after your left-of-field
encounter, that's angels. If you feel less fear
and trust yourself less. But beware
of other voices, easier to bear
which sound more like angels than angels do
but leave you in turmoil, saying 'More. More. More.'

8 In Memory of Katherine James

Killed September 11, 2001

You can believe that God exists
but the devil's a way of talking. Yes,
except that demons are us in disguise
as angel voices. They never surprise
but confirm our hatreds. We easily miss
that they're nonsense messages, an excuse
to megaphone the ego's madness.

She was a musician, so was used
to leaving her body and strolling through
the wide avenues and sunny porticoes
that melody built. She had an ear
for what was beyond herself, was more
than her wishes. Therefore, I hear
her lovely harmonics in that terrible roar.

9 Angel of Dying

'A young boy dying on a ward in Kabul
wouldn't stop singing – made music from screams,
wouldn't sleep, wouldn't drink, but chanted dreams
in ferocious head notes. He frightened us all
but held his dying like a torch of flame
for us to follow. Arches leapt darkly overhead,
threw shadows over us. He led

on past comfort, past reason or blame
with the terrible energy of the dead
whose death is more life than flesh can bear,
a birth, not an ending. This truth tore
the living to pieces. Then silence sang of him instead...
I've never forgotten him. No, don't ask
about dying. How to live is the task.'

10 Angel of Healing

Every disease is a work of art
if you play it rightly. Of course, it hurts
like hell, but can be used
as a reminder that your mind
is not on its business, which is 'now',
however painful. Novalis knew
that all illness requires a musical cure.

By this he meant: whatever the form
imposed by arthritis, or by the gout,
your job's to compose yourself round about
its formal restrictions, and make that sing,
even to death. And all that pain?
Messengers from your beloved to say
'Wait for me, darling, I'm on my way!'

11 The Good, the Bad and the Complex

In angel orders there are twelve degrees
of chaos. Nonsense; then scramble;
raving that's modified into scat.
The sleeping orders' psychedelic dreams
give rise to cities, till they wake
and trigger a local apocalypse.
There are angels of breakdown, and collapse

is their specialist subject. Angels of decline,
angels of entropy. Then angels who tell
you what to do when (that's close to hell);
angels pedantic, angels of the Law.
The Complex orders know what chaos is for –
that's for self-forgetting – and, greatest of all,
is the Angel of Not Knowing a Thing Any More.

12 Christ as Angel of the Will of God

What would it be to move beyond
our need for angels? Just to relax
might take us a century. To like
that sensation, longer. We'd understand
and calculate the logarithms of grace
to easy solutions in our sleep.
Not to need messages about
but to be, instead, a literal place

we have a map for? Because it's here:
a murderous waste ground. To be free
to gather bouquets of nettles? to be
those passionate kisses? that hot pain?
Not to mind hurting because you see
Christ bringing cool dock leaves of mercy.

Gwyneth Lewis was born in Cardiff. After reading English at Cambridge, she went to America as a Harkness Fellow, studying at Harvard and Columbia, before going to Oxford to write a doctoral thesis on the 18th-century Welsh literary forger, Iolo Morganwg. After periods as a journalist in New York and the Philippines, she returned to Cardiff, where she worked for many years as a television producer. She is now a freelance writer.

Keeping Mum (Bloodaxe Books, 2003) is her sixth book of poetry. Her first in English, *Parables & Faxes* (Bloodaxe Books, 1995), won the Aldeburgh Poetry Festival Prize and was shortlisted for a Forward Prize, as was her second, *Zero Gravity* (Bloodaxe Books, 1998). The BBC made a documentary from the title-sequence of *Zero Gravity*, which was inspired by her astronaut cousin's Space Shuttle mission. Both *Zero Gravity* and *Keeping Mum* are Poetry Book Society Recommendations.

Her poetry books in Welsh are *Sonedau Redsa* (Gwasg Gomer, 1990), *Cyfrif Un ac Un yn Dri* (Cyhoeddiadau Barddas, 1996), and *Y Llofrudd Iaith* (Cyhoeddiadau Barddas, 1999), winner of the Welsh Arts Council Book of the Year Prize.

In 2001 she was awarded a Fellowship by NESTA and is currently living and travelling on a boat. In 2002 she published *Sunbathing in the Rain: A Cheerful Book about Depression* (Flamingo), her first book of prose.